OLD HU-HU

Kyle Mewburn

illustrated by Rachel Driscoll

SCHOLASTIC
AUCKLAND SYDNEY NEW YORK LONDON TORONTO
MEXICO CITY NEW DELHI HONG KONG

Old Hu-Hu flew
to the moon
and back.

Then fell to the ground.

Dead.

What a silly thing to do!
To fly all the way to the moon!

And yet...

wasn't that *exactly*
the kind of thing
Old Hu-Hu used to do
all the time,
long ago,
when he was young?

Maybe he forgot
he was old?

Insects came
from far and wide
to say goodbye.

Some flew,
four wings and two.

Some crawled,
six legs and eight,
or no legs at all.

Everyone loved Old Hu-Hu.

But nobody loved him quite as much as little Hu-Hu-Tu.

Maybe that's why Hu-Hu-Tu
was the only one who knew
that it *wasn't* Old Hu-Hu,
lying upside down
on the ground.

It was just an empty shell.

But if that were true ...
where *was* Old Hu-Hu?

"Where's Old Hu-Hu?"
Ladybird laughed.

"Why, he's sitting on a cloud
with all his old friends,
munching and laughing -
a young Hu-Hu grub again!"

Could it really be true?
Was *that* where Old Hu-Hu
had got to?

Across the sky
Hu-Hu-Tu flew,
calling:
"Old Hu-Hu! Old Hu-Hu!
Where are you?"

But there came no reply
as the cold wind blew.

"Where's Old Hu-Hu?"
Spider cried.

"What a silly question!
Just look around!
There's some of him here.
There's more of him there.
His blood is in the soil.
His breath is in the air.
I can see him in the flowers.
I can see him in your hair.
Old Hu-Hu's not gone!
He's everywhere!"

Could it really be true?
If he looked really hard
would he see Old Hu-Hu?

Low and high
searched Hu-Hu-Tu,
asking:
"Old Hu-Hu! Old Hu-Hu!
Is that *really* you?"

But there came no reply
as the dark shadows grew.

"Old Hu-Hu's not *really* dead,"
Butterfly said.

"But his time as our friend
has come to an end.
Soon he'll awake,
born once again!
He might be an elephant,
a snake, or a hen."

Could it really be true?
When Old Hu-Hu woke up
would he start life anew?

By Old Hu-Hu's side
sat Hu-Hu-Tu,
whispering:
"Old Hu-Hu! Old Hu-Hu!
Wake up, won't you?"

But there came no reply
as the night soaked with dew.

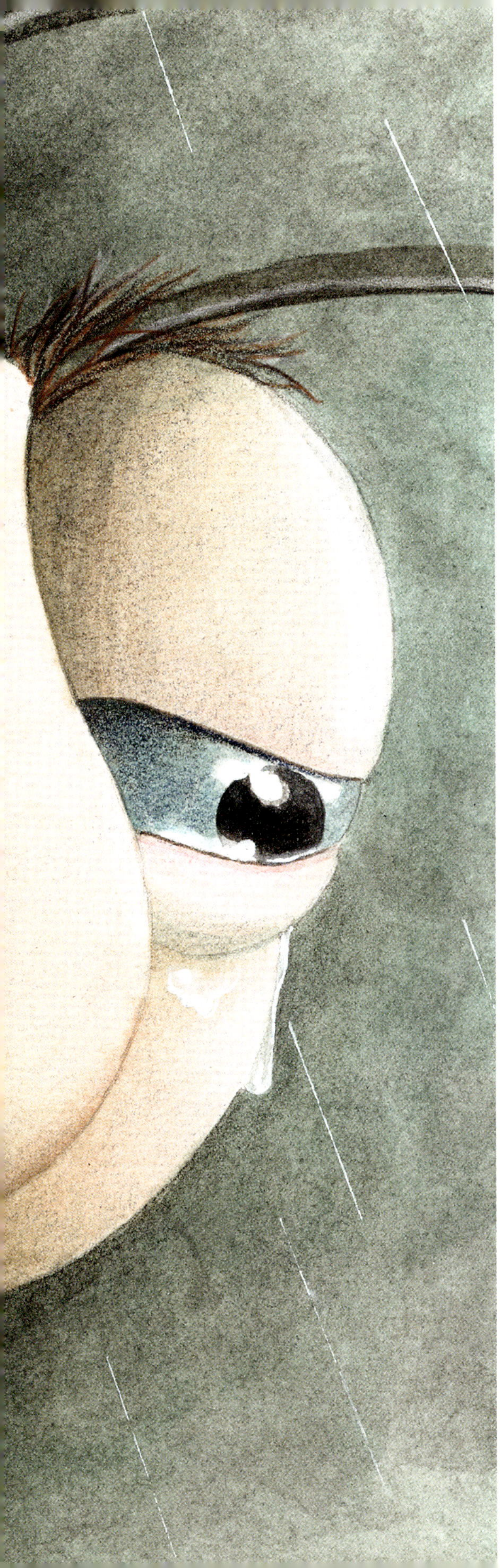

It was no use!
Old Hu-Hu
was gone
forever.

"And I never said goodbye!"
Hu-Hu-Tu cried.

He cried
and cried
the whole night through.

"If only I knew
where Old Hu-Hu got to!"

But then...

as the sun cracked open the sky,
he heard Old Hu-Hu's voice.

As clear as day.

"Hu-Hu-Tu,
the day is new!
So what are *you*
going to do?"

Hu-Hu-Tu couldn't believe his ears.

"Old Hu-Hu! Old Hu-Hu!"
he called. "Where are you?"

He listened again.

Old Hu-Hu's voice
wasn't coming
from the clouds,
or the dirt,
or the flowers.

It was coming
from inside
Hu-Hu-Tu!

At last he knew.

"*That's* where you got to," smiled Hu-Hu-Tu.

Hu-Hu-Tu flew
to the moon
and back.

Just like Old Hu-Hu
used to do,
all the time,
long ago,
when he was young ...

just like Hu-Hu-Tu.

For Momo, who forgot she was old too – KM

For my parents and little Sophie too – RD & MG

First published in 2009 by Scholastic New Zealand Limited
Private Bag 94407, Greenmount, Manukau 2141, New Zealand

Scholastic Australia Pty Limited
PO Box 579, Gosford, NSW 2250, Australia

Text © Kyle Mewburn, 2009
Illustrations © Rachel Driscoll, 2009

ISBN 978-1-86943-921-7

All rights reserved. No part of this publication may be reproduced or transmitted in any form or by any means, electronic, mechanical or digital, including photocopying, recording, storage in any information retrieval system, or otherwise, without prior written permission of the publisher.

National Library of New Zealand Cataloguing-in-Publication Data

Mewburn, Kyle.
Old Hu-hu / Kyle Mewburn.
ISBN 978-1-86943-897-5 (hbk.)—978-1-86943-921-7 (pbk.)
[1. Death—Fiction. 2. Bereavement—Fiction.] I. Driscoll, Rachel.
II. Title.
NZ823.2—dc 22

Illustrations created in pencil, paint and tears
Publishing team: Christine Dale, Penny Scown and Annette Bisman
Designed by Michael Greenfield and typeset in Old Hu-Hu
Printed in Malaysia by TWP Sdn Bhd